D0516491

DISCOVERING WALT

The Magical Life of Walt Disney

by

Jean-Pierre Isbouts

A ROUNDTABLE PRESS BOOK

New York

EDITIONS

A Roundtable Press Book
New York

EDITIONS

Printed in China

For information, address
Disney Editions, 114 Fifth Avenue, New York, NY 10011

For Disney Editions
Editorial Director: Wendy Lefkon
Design Director: Elliot Kreloff
Senior Editor: Sara Baysinger
Assistant Editor: Jody Revenson

For Roundtable Press, Inc.
Directors: Julie Merberg, Susan E. Meyer, Marsha Melnick
Design: pink design, inc.
Editor: John Glenn

ISBN 0-7868-5354-9

First Edition

2 4 6 8 10 9 7 5 3 1

CONTENTS

THE MAGIC OF WALT DISNEY

One summer day in the late 1940s, a young boy visited the new Disney studio in Burbank. As he walked around, he bumped into the man who had created all the wonderful characters the boy knew so well: Snow White, Pinocchio, and, of course, Mickey Mouse. The name of the man was Walt Disney. He was a fairly tall man with an open, friendly face, a small mustache, and a ready smile.

Mickey reads to Pluto in
The Pointer (1939).

The little boy wondered if he could ask Mr. Disney a question. "Sure, go ahead," Walt said. "Do you still draw Mickey Mouse?" asked the boy. Walt shook his head and said, "No, not anymore." There were now many artists, called animators, who

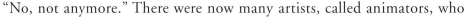

drew the characters. "Do you come up with the ideas and the jokes in the Mickey Mouse cartoons?" the boy asked. Walt sighed and said, no, he didn't do that anymore, either. The little boy paused, and said, "Well then, Mr. Disney, just what do you do?" Walt smiled and thought for a moment. "Sometimes I think of myself as a little bee," he said. "I go from one area of the studio to another and gather pollen and sort of stimulate everybody. I guess that's the job I do."

The opening screen for the "Walt Disney Presents" TV series (1958–1961)

4

All his life, Walt wanted to entertain people—to take them from the worries of everyday life and bring them into a magical world of fantasy. First, he did so by creating short animated cartoons, and then he moved on to a series of feature-length cartoons, starting with *Snow White and the Seven Dwarfs*.

Had Walt made only animated films, he would still have been famous. But he kept pushing forward: He began to make movies with live actors and films about nature and wildlife. Then he decided he wanted to build a park where parents and their children could go and have fun together. This idea grew into Disneyland.

Today, Walt Disney Studio continues to produce magic with wonderful animated films such as *The Little Mermaid* and *The Lion King*. Disneyland still draws large crowds every year, and more Disney theme parks have been built in Orlando, Florida; Tokyo, Japan; and Paris, France. Each year, millions of children are entertained by hundreds of characters and their unique "Disney Magic."

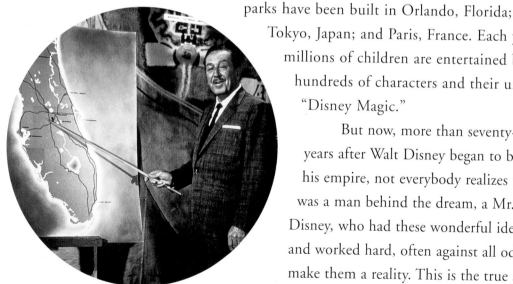

Walt presents his plans for EPCOT in "the EPCOT film" (1966), created to explain his vision to Disney employees.

But now, more than seventy-five years after Walt Disney began to build his empire, not everybody realizes there was a man behind the dream, a Mr. Walt Disney, who had these wonderful ideas and worked hard, often against all odds, to make them a reality. This is the true story of Walt Disney, and how he created the timeless wonder of Disney entertainment.

Chapter 1

WALT'S FAMILY

Walt's first home on Tripp Avenue in Chicago

Walter Elias Disney was born in Chicago on December 5, 1901. His parents, Elias and Flora, had been married in Florida on New Year's Day, 1888. Before Walt was born, they had three boys: Raymond, Herbert, and Roy, who were spaced roughly two years apart. When Walt was born, Roy was eight years old. The Disney family had moved to Chicago at a time when that city was a fast-growing, exciting place.

A carpenter and contractor, Elias built the house his family lived in with his own hands. He also built other homes in the area, as well as a new church for his good friend, the Reverend Walter Parr.

In early 1901, Flora told Elias she was pregnant with their fourth child. As it happened, the wife of Reverend Parr was expecting a baby, too. One night over dinner, Elias and his friend struck a deal: If Elias had a son, he'd name him Walter, after the reverend. And if Reverend Parr had a son, he'd name him Elias. When Flora gave birth to a baby boy, Elias kept his promise and named him Walter Elias Disney—Walt, for short. Reverend Parr, however, did not uphold his end of the deal, naming his baby Charles Alexander!

Two years after Walt was born, Flora gave birth to Ruth, the baby girl she had wanted for so long. Close in age, and much younger than their big brothers, Walt and Ruth would become constant childhood playmates.

* * * * * * * *

Elias's business was doing well enough to support their family of seven, but he and Flora were concerned that Chicago was not a safe place to raise their children. Then, one day in 1906, the police arrested two local boys for killing a policeman. When violence hit this close to home, Elias decided that he had had enough of big city life. Elias's brother Robert owned some property in Marceline, Missouri, a small farming town. Robert suggested that his brother's family join him there to live and work on a farm. So when Walt was only four years old, he and his family made the 312-mile trip southwest from Chicago to Marceline, Missouri.

Walt's baptismal certificate

Walt was an eager-looking baby, with wide, curious eyes.

"They were waiting for a girl when Walter arrived," explained Ruth, pictured here with her older brother Walt. "But they had to wait for me!"

Chapter 2

ON THE FARM IN MARCELINE

Ruth and Walt in Marceline

For the next six years, the farm in Marceline would be Walt's universe. He loved the view of endless fields of wheat and barley, the fresh morning dew on the grass, and the sweet smell of apple blossoms in springtime. In the fall, the same trees would grow heavy with crispy red Wolf River apples, so big that people came from miles around to see them. Walt had fond memories of this lush, green landscape and a lawn shaded by weeping willows.

He also loved the community spirit of farm life—the way neighbors helped neighbors, whether fixing fences or sharing food. Above all, he loved the farm animals: horses, cows, chickens, and pigs.

While the farm was a playground for Walt and Ruth, it was a very different experience for his older brothers. Farmwork requires many hands, and Elias couldn't afford to hire any. So his three oldest sons, Herbert, Ray, and Roy, put in long hours, sweating under the sweltering Missouri sun as they tried to get the most out of every acre of land the family owned. When Herbert and Ray asked if they could get some pay for their hard work, Elias refused. The family was just scraping by, Elias explained, and he felt his boys should help out for the good of the whole family. Elias's stern attitude frustrated his sons.

While Elias instilled in Walt a strong work ethic and spirit of adventure, Flora gave Walt his sense of humor. "My mother had a terrific sense of humor," Walt recalled. Flora was also much more easygoing than Elias. "We could always get anything we wanted out of our mother. And she'd even connive with us against our dad," Walt explained.

Flora and Elias Disney in 1913

When Flora's homemade butter became a big hit in the town—and the local grocery store began to stock and sell it—Elias decided that his family shouldn't eat up the profits. So Flora would butter her children's bread—but serve them the slices upside down so that Elias never knew.

* * * * * * * *

Walt's family played an important role in his early years and in shaping the man he became. Walt's uncle Mike Martin was an engineer on the Santa Fe Railroad. The train track ran straight through the town of Marceline.

Whenever Uncle Mike was in the front cab, he would blow the horn and the children in town would come out and wave. The sight of a huge locomotive chugging away, right in front of him, instilled in Walt a lifelong love of trains.

Walt's aunt Margaret helped spark Walt's artistic side. Whenever she came to visit her nephew, she would bring him crayons and paper. He, in turn, would make wonderful pictures for his aunt.

* * * * * * * *

Aunt Margaret, Elias's sister-in-law

Walt didn't start school until 1909, when he was seven years old, "because there was nobody to take me to school," he explained. His mother had to stay home and take care of little Ruth. So Flora and Elias decided to keep him out of school until she could go, too. This didn't make Walt happy: "It was the most embarrassing thing that can happen to a fellow, that I had to practically start in school with my little sister, Ruth, who was two years younger!"

When Walt did begin at the local Park School, his grades weren't very good. His attention often wandered to things he found more interesting, like drawing.

Meanwhile, Herbert and Ray, who were in their late teens, decided they'd had enough of farm life. One spring night in 1908, they crawled out of their bedroom window and left for Chicago.

Herbert Disney, Walt's second-oldest brother, around 1914

After the boys ran away, Elias and Roy had to work even harder. Then, in the fall of 1910, Elias fell ill. His head throbbed, his throat burned, and his fever was alarmingly high. The doctor said he had typhoid, which in those days could be deadly. Flora nursed her husband at home because there were no hospitals nearby.

After two dangerous months, Elias finally recovered, but he wasn't nearly as strong as he'd been before the illness. Knowing that he'd never again have the strength for the hard work on the farm, he decided to sell it. And so the Disney family packed up and moved to Kansas City.

Chapter 3

HARD WORK IN KANSAS CITY

Walt's older brother and lifelong partner Roy, in Kansas City around 1913

Walt's family arrived in Kansas City in 1911. They eventually settled in a house at 3028 Bellefontaine Avenue. Elias decided to purchase a newspaper delivery business with the understanding that Roy and Walt would be his "employees." Walt was just nine years old, but he had to get up every morning by 4:00 A.M. to deliver the newspapers before it was time to go to school.

Many other newspaper delivery services used a horse and wagon, but Elias used pushcarts, which were cheaper, though much harder to use. On Sundays, when the paper was much thicker, the tiring job became even more difficult. "Our pushcarts weren't big enough for Sunday papers, so we had to take two loads out and then come all the way back to the distribution point and take two more loads," Walt remembered.

For six long years, Walt and Roy delivered the newspapers every single day of the week. It was especially hard in winter, when it was cold and slippery outside. Walt would get so sleepy it was a constant struggle to stay awake. Walt was a tough child, but sometimes the cold, lonely mornings got to him. At those times, Walt was grateful for one thing: "There was no one around, so I could cry."

The Disney House on Bellefontaine Avenue in Kansas City, around 1915

A serious-looking Walt in Kansas City around 1913

Elias's customers were more important than his sons' comfort: Elias insisted that Walt and Roy place the newspapers inside the storm doors, rather than throwing them onto the lawn as other newsboys did. Elias could be tough on his boys, and sometimes hit them. This was not unusual behavior for parents when Walt was growing up. As Walt's daughter Diane explains, "Elias was probably not too much out of style for patriarchs of his day. He sounds a little tough to us now, but he just wanted to keep that family together, keep them good, keep the boys out of trouble, and get them going down the right road."

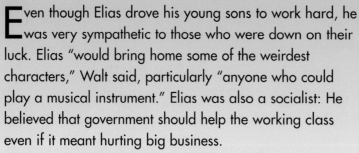

ELIAS

Elias and Flora, sometime in the 1920s

Even though Elias drove his young sons to work hard, he was very sympathetic to those who were down on their luck. Elias "would bring home some of the weirdest characters," Walt said, particularly "anyone who could play a musical instrument." Elias was also a socialist: He believed that government should help the working class even if it meant hurting big business.

Known for his thrift, Elias also had a soft spot when it came to supporting his children's passion for the arts. When Ruth showed an interest in music, Elias bought her an expensive player piano. Similarly, when Walt wanted art lessons, his dad readily agreed.

Still, the hard work took its toll. Walt didn't do very well at school. He was often just too tired to pay attention. But sometimes he would be inspired. On one occasion, he memorized the Gettysburg Address and came to school dressed as Abraham Lincoln. The school principal was so impressed that he took Walt to every class for a performance.

* * * * * * * *

As he entered his teenage years, Walt became close friends with a boy named Walt Pfeiffer. The Pfeiffer home was always filled with laughter and music. The Pfeiffers took Walt to local vaudeville shows and to see Charlie Chaplin movies at the cinema. Going to the theater and movies opened up a whole new world for Walt. He memorized the vaudeville jokes, and Walt and Walt Pfeiffer started a stage act of their own—"The Two Walts"—which was quite a hit in the neighborhood.

Walt was having such a good time in Kansas City that when Elias announced that the family would be moving back to Chicago, Walt wanted to stay behind. So in the summer of 1917, Elias took Flora and Ruth to Chicago and began his new job as head of construction at the O-Zell Company (a jelly firm that he had invested in). Walt remained in Kansas City for the summer with his brother Roy, who was then twenty-four years old. Walt was happy to be rid of the newspaper route and eager to see a bit of the world. Roy arranged for him to become a "news butcher." A news butcher sold soda pop, magazines, and candy to passengers on the train. Walt loved every minute of it, and he adored riding the big trains—so much so that he often forgot about selling his wares.

Chapter 4

THE GREAT WAR IN EUROPE

Walt (right) and his friend Russell Maas show off their new uniforms.

When summer was over, Walt joined his family in Chicago and enrolled as a freshman at McKinley High School, where he drew cartoons for the school newspaper. At night, he took art lessons at the Chicago Institute of Art.

That fall, when President Woodrow Wilson decided that the United States would join Britain and France in the "Great War" against Germany, thousands of young Americans—including Roy and Herbert—volunteered to fight overseas. Walt wanted to go to war as well, but at sixteen he was too young. When he heard that the Red Cross would take seventeen-year-olds to drive ambulances in France, he changed the birth date on his passport application from "1901" to "1900." With a passport that made him seventeen, Walt was accepted as an ambulance driver. He shipped out to France in late 1918, just after the war ended.

Embroidered cards Walt sent to his parents while serving with the Red Cross Ambulance Corps in France

Throughout 1919, Walt drove an ambulance, played poker, and wrote long letters home. He also started smoking. In his time off, he made extra money by painting helmets in camouflage colors, then banging them up to make them look as if they had been in a real battle. Soldiers bought these helmets to bring home as souvenirs.

At year's end, Walt returned home. He no longer thought of himself as a kid from Missouri. He was a grown man who had been to France and seen the world.

Chapter 5

WALT'S FIRST CARTOONS

hen Walt returned to his family in Chicago, Elias found a job for his son at the O-Zell factory. But Walt informed his father that he didn't want a factory job; he wanted to become an artist. Elias didn't approve. He had supported Walt's art education, but getting a job as an artist sounded like a crazy idea.

Still, Walt had made up his mind. So he left his parents' home in Chicago and went back to Kansas City. There, he moved in with his brother Herbert, Herbert's wife, Louise, and their little daughter, Dorothy, in the old Disney house on Bellefontaine Avenue. Roy, who had just been discharged from the navy, joined them as well.

First, Walt tried to get work as an artist for the *Kansas City Star*, but they wouldn't even hire him as a truck driver. Big brother Roy came

Walt drew this caricature of himself and his father around 1919.

Walt's oldest brother, Herbert, and his wife, Louise, pictured in Ruth's *Golden School Days* book

Walt's early letterhead

through, though, with the suggestion that he try to get a job at the Pesmen-Rubin Commercial Art studio. Pesmen-Rubin made advertisements, and Walt was asked to bring in samples of his work. So he showed them some sketches he'd made in France and was hired on the spot. At Pesmen-Rubin, Walt met a quiet young man named Ub Iwerks, who would become very important to Walt as the years rolled on. In the meantime, both Ub and Walt were put to work, making catalogues for farm equipment.

When he got the job, he rushed to tell his aunt Margaret the good news—that he was being paid to draw pictures. Sadly, Auntie Margaret was ill at the time and didn't get as excited as Walt thought she would.

Shortly before Christmas, business got bad, and Walt and his friend Ub were both laid off. So they decided to go into business together. They called their company Iwerks-Disney, because Disney-Iwerks sounded like a company that made eyeglasses. Unfortunately, they couldn't make enough money to stay in business for very long. So when Walt was offered a job in February 1920 at the Kansas City Film

Walt (center) with two of his first animator friends, Ub Iwerks (left) and Fred Harman (right)

Ad Company for $40 a week (a good salary in those days), they agreed he should take it. Ub joined him there a few weeks later.

Walt at the drawing table at Kansas City Film Ad

UB IWERKS

Kansas City was just the first stop in a long, productive friendship and working relationship between Ub Iwerks and Walt. In 1924, Ub followed Walt to Hollywood, where he became a partner in the Disney Brothers Studio.

Ub's strengths were artistic. He was an extraordinarily gifted (and speedy) animator. Ub was able to turn out some seven hundred drawings a day. Today, a skilled animator usually produces around one hundred drawings in a week.

In 1930, Ub would take a chance to start his own studio, producing a series called *Flip the Frog*. Although Ub's shorts were well animated, he didn't have Walt's gift for storytelling and humor. *Flip the Frog* never became as popular as Walt's cartoons.

Walt and Ub, around 1929

In 1940, Ub would return to the Disney studio. Walt's old friend eventually became an expert in special effects. Ub won two Academy Awards for his inventions, one of which made it easier for studios to put live actors and animated characters together in one scene.

It was at Kansas City Film Ad that Walt was first introduced to animated films—cartoons. They were still very primitive. Walt was told to put small, pinned cutouts of a character on a board, under a film camera. He would move the limbs slightly, shoot a frame, move the limbs again, and so forth. When you ran the film, this would create the illusion of real movement—just like a flip book. Walt had seen animated cartoons made in New York that used a series of drawings—rather than cutouts—each in a slightly different position than the last. To him, these animated drawings were much more lifelike.

Elias's "car barn," where Walt carried out early experiments with animation

To learn more about animation, Walt went to the Kansas City Library and read every book he could find on the subject. He then borrowed a camera from his employer and created a makeshift studio in the garage Elias had built behind the Disney home.

In time, he began to produce real cartoons by drawing a series of characters in different positions. And his characters would perform some of the funny gags Walt remembered from the vaudeville shows he'd seen in high school.

After he'd finished several short cartoons ("shorts"), he showed the reel to the owner of the local Newman Theater, who ordered a new cartoon for every week. Walt called his shorts "Newman Laugh-O-grams." Each reel was intended to carry advertisements, but Walt always tried to make them funny.

While Walt was having a great time learning new ways to create cartoons, things were not going so well for Elias. The O-Zell Company went bankrupt. Elias moved back to Kansas City with Flora and Ruth. The Disney house now held eight people. And though it wasn't a big place, it was a reasonably happy time. Walt enjoyed being surrounded by family.

An opening screen used for one of the Laugh-O-grams

Within months of Elias's return in 1921, Roy fell ill with tuberculosis. That disease was very fearsome at the time—and very contagious. So Roy was sent away to a special hospital in Arizona for tuberculosis patients. Then Herbert got notice from the Postal Service, where he worked, that he and his family were being transferred to Portland, Oregon. Elias and Flora decided to sell the house and go to Portland with him. The Disney home—so full of family only weeks before—was drained of the loving sounds to which Walt had become accustomed.

Walt's sister, Ruth, remembered that, on the day he took his family to the train station for a tearful good-bye, "he couldn't keep his face straight. He suddenly turned and left. He was upset. He realized, I know, that he was going to be alone then."

Walt found a room in a rooming house, and he made up his mind to start his own animation company. He raised some $15,000 from investors, quit his job, and on May 23, 1922, founded Laugh-O-gram Films. He was only twenty years old. Soon, Ub Iwerks and five other animators joined him.

Laugh-O-gram was a fun place to work. Walt and his team felt that they were at the forefront of a new form of entertainment. As his first project, he decided to make a series of cartoons based on classic fairy tales. He made a deal with a company called Pictorial Clubs, which promised to distribute the films to theaters. At the same time, Walt also became the Kansas City correspondent for Universal Films, shooting newsreel footage

Roy Disney relaxes in a
Kansas City park.

of any news events that took place in the area.

Unfortunately, Pictorial Clubs went out of business before it could pay Walt for the cartoons he had made, and Walt had nobody to distribute the cartoons he'd completed. Since he had used up his investors' money to make the cartoons, Walt had nothing left to pay the rent. As he later recalled, "I moved into the studio. I slept on a bunch of old canvas and cushions on the chairs. And there was no bath there, so once a week I'd go to the Union Station and go in; for a dime, I could get a bath."

Fortunately, Roy hadn't forgotten about his little brother. Every now and then, Walt would receive a letter which said, "Kid, I haven't heard from you, but I just have a suspicion you could use a little money. I am enclosing a check. Fill it out in any amount up to $30." And so, Walt said, "I'd always write $30 on the check."

Even when he was living on canned beans, Walt didn't give up. He got a job making a film about dental hygiene for a local dentist, who gave him the grand sum of $500. Did Walt save the money? No. Did he move back into a real apartment or start to eat well? No. Instead, he decided to create a whole new kind of cartoon, which would cost him every penny he had.

Walt clowns around
in Kansas City's
Swope Park.

Walt directing Virginia Davis as Alice. "I thought he was just terrific," said Virginia years later. "I think he was probably my first love. And he told so many stories, it was great fun."

A scene from *Alice's Wonderland* in which a live Alice rides an animated elephant

His idea was to put a real, live person in an animated world. He named the new cartoon *Alice's Wonderland*, and he asked a local four-year-old, Virginia Davis, to play the part. Walt filmed the little girl in her parents' home and against a big white screen, and later he and his animators added the animated characters. But before Walt could finish the film, he ran out of money again.

By July 1923, Laugh-O-gram was out of business and Walt had sold his movie camera. All he had left was a cardboard suitcase, a change of clothes, and an unfinished film reel of *Alice's Wonderland*. But rather than giving up, Walt decided to go where all the moviemakers go: Hollywood.

Chapter 6

A STUDIO IN HOLLYWOOD

The young director at work

"It was a big day, the day I got on that Santa Fe Limited and came to Hollywood," Walt remembered. "I was just free and happy. But I'd failed. I think it's important to have a good hard failure when you're young. I came to Hollywood and there was just one thing I wanted to do. I wanted to get into the motion picture business. I wanted to be a director."

Walt moved in with his 62-year-old uncle Robert, Elias's brother, who had moved to the West Coast a few years earlier. As soon as he was settled in, he knocked on every studio door in town looking for work. Although he was ready to take any job, they all turned him down. Soon, Walt realized that the only way to break into the film business was to do what he did best: making cartoons. Uncle Robert let Walt turn his garage into a tiny studio.

Walt sent the unfinished reel of *Alice's Wonderland* to a New York cartoon distributor named Margaret Winkler, proposing to make a whole series of Alice cartoons for her. Amazingly, she accepted—and agreed to pay Walt $1,500 apiece for six Alice cartoons.

Walt was elated, but he quickly realized he couldn't do it by himself. He needed a partner to take care of the money matters. Roy was the only logical choice. Fortunately, Roy was healthy again, recovering from tuberculosis in a nearby hospital. Walt jumped on the bus, barged into the hospital, and told

Roy about his good fortune and his idea that he and Roy should go into business. The next day, Roy left the hospital for good, and Disney Brothers Studios was born.

Roy rented a vacant lot on Hollywood Boulevard for all the exterior scenes, while Walt bought a secondhand camera for $200. They set up shop in a small store at 4649 Kingswell Avenue. By February 1924, the *Alice* series was in full production, which means that filming was underway. A few months later, Ub Iwerks joined them.

Walt convinced the parents of his young star, Virginia Davis, to move from Kansas City to Los Angeles so that she could star in the new series. Virginia recalls that working with Walt was a

Walt (second from left) and Roy (behind the camera) direct Virginia Davis in *Alice's Spooky Adventure*, as her father (far left) looks on.

dream for a little girl. Since the films were silent, Walt could give Virginia instructions as she went along. "Act like you're running," he'd tell her, or, "Now look back and look scared."

Meanwhile, the studio needed someone to help with inking and painting the cartoon drawings. A young woman from Idaho named Lillian Bounds applied for and got the job, at $15 per week. At night,

Lillian Bounds, Walt's future wife, and the rest of the Disney Brothers staff outside the Kingswell Avenue office

Lilly as
a little girl

Walt usually drove his female employees home in a used pickup truck. He always made a point of dropping Lillian off last. During their time alone in the truck, Lillian would tell Walt all about her life as the youngest of ten children, and about her father, who had been a blacksmith.

At the time, Walt was living with his brother Roy in a small room they rented near their studio. But working and living together began to wear on the two brothers. Meanwhile, Roy had been pining for his Kansas City girlfriend, Edna Francis. The two had planned to marry four years earlier, but Roy's illness had intervened. Roy sent her a telegram and asked her to join him in Los Angeles—and be his wife. She accepted. On April 11, 1925, Roy and Edna were married at Uncle Robert's house in Los Angeles. Walt was there, in a new suit—and so was Lilly.

Newlyweds Roy
and Edna in 1925

With Roy and Edna engaged, Walt decided to take the big step as well. He asked Lilly if she would marry him. As Lilly remembered the day, "After he had proposed to me, he said, 'I can buy you an engagement ring, or I can make a down payment on a car. Which will you have?' I don't remember what I said, but he has always told everybody that I said the car, because he bought the car first." Walt loved his fancy automobile—it was called a Moon roadster and was manufactured in St. Louis.

Walt and Lilly were married on July 13, 1925, in her brother's house in Lewiston, Idaho. Her niece Marjorie recalled that Lilly giggled throughout the wedding: "Oh, Aunt Lilly, whenever she'd get nervous she would giggle."

After the wedding, the couple took a romantic honeymoon trip to Mount Rainier in Washington state.

At around this time, Walt and Roy began to build a new studio on Hyperion Avenue in Los Angeles. Business was growing as Walt developed new episodes of the *Alice* series. Rather than drawing himself, Walt now supervised a growing team of animators. While his animators created the many drawings necessary to bring the cartoons to life, Walt focused on the storylines of Alice's adventures and the playful gags between Alice and the animated characters.

In the meantime, Margaret Winkler had turned over her distribution company to her husband, Charlie Mintz. Although he ordered eighteen more *Alice* episodes, Mintz was far more demanding than his wife had ever been. He always pushed Walt to create funnier gags and more exciting visual effects.

In 1927, the head of Universal Studios, Carl Laemmle, suggested to Mintz that he develop a new series with an animated rabbit as the main character. Mintz told Walt to drop the *Alice* series and start work on a new one. The new character was called Oswald the Lucky Rabbit. The audience loved the little rabbit, and soon the

Walt and Lilly honeymooning at Mount Rainier

Walt and child actress Margie Gay, who played Alice in many of the later *Alice* episodes

name Oswald appeared on the marquees of film theaters, next to the title of the main attraction.

At this time, Walt and Roy decided that the name of the studio should be changed from Disney Brothers to the Walt Disney Studio. In later years, some animators would grumble that, whatever they did, Walt would always get the credit. But giving the company a strong identification with one individual was a smart business move. Roy knew that people would always hear the name Walt Disney and think of wonderful entertainment.

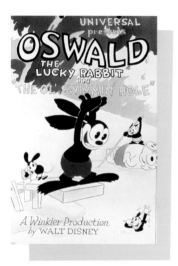

A poster for *The Ol' Swimmin' Hole*, starring Oswald the Lucky Rabbit

With the money from the *Oswald* series, Roy and Walt decided to buy real homes for their new families. They bought adjoining lots on Lyric Avenue and built two identical homes. Lilly's mother moved in with Walt and Lilly. To round out their little home, Walt decided to surprise Lilly with a little chow puppy for Christmas. And sure enough, the dog became part of the family. "From that time on, it was her baby . . . . She wouldn't let it out of her sight. It had to sleep in our bedroom," said Walt.

The sun was shining on Walt, both in his home life and in business. He had married the woman he loved, and he and Roy lived in relative comfort. Disney relatives dropped by to admire their new prosperity. Life was good. Oswald the Lucky Rabbit had, indeed, proven to be lucky.

At least for a while.

Lilly, Walt, and their pet chow, Sunnee

Chapter 7

MICKEY MOUSE AND FRIENDS

In February 1928, the contract for *Oswald the Lucky Rabbit* was up for renewal. Together with Lilly, Walt boarded a train to New York to strike a new deal with Charlie Mintz. But Mintz had an unpleasant surprise in store. He had secretly offered Walt's staff more money and freedom if they came to work for him instead of Walt. Most of the studio staff—with the exception of Ub Iwerks—had accepted. Walt realized that there was little he could do, because, legally, Oswald belonged to Mintz, not to him. That was an important lesson that Walt never forgot. From then on, Walt made sure that all the characters and stories he developed always remained the property of the Walt Disney Studio.

But Walt didn't hold a grudge against Charlie Mintz. As Walt boarded the train for the return trip to Los Angeles, he knew he needed to come up with a new idea, fast. He was gazing out the train window and started thinking about a mouse—like the little mouse that used to crawl across his drawing board, back in Kansas City.

A birthday card Walt sent to Flora in the mid-1920s shows a cartoon mouse.

Walt and Lilly. Lilly inked and painted Ub Iwerks' early Mickey Mouse drawings along with her sister, Hazel, and sister-in-law, Edna.

Walt took a piece of paper and drew the head of a mouse with big round ears. He showed it to Lilly and asked for her opinion. Lilly liked it. "I think I will call him Mortimer Mouse," Walt said. Lilly looked more closely at the picture and said, "No, I don't like 'Mortimer.'" She thought for a moment, then suggested, "How about Mickey?" Walt mulled it over and agreed. Mickey Mouse was born by the time Walt returned to Los Angeles.

Walt showed his Mickey sketches to Ub Iwerks. Ub then began to make drawings for a new cartoon called *Plane Crazy*. When Walt showed the new cartoon to distributors, they were not impressed. All things being equal, Mickey Mouse didn't look much different from Oswald the Lucky Rabbit or other popular characters of that time, like Felix the Cat.

A scene from *Plane Crazy*, which Ub Iwerks drew in secrecy, because Walt didn't want his departing staffers to find out about Mickey Mouse

Walt knew that he had to think of something new and special, in order to get his mouse into theaters. Ever since the 1927 release of *The Jazz Singer*, the first major film with synchronized sound, everyone in Hollywood was excited about this new technology. Up until then, all motion pictures had been silent, with organists or pianists providing background music in the movie theater.

Walt's idea was to bring sound to his cartoons. Others had tried to do so already, but no one had done it very well. Walt decided that a Mickey cartoon called *Steamboat Willie* would be produced with music and sound effects. This was a big risk—nobody knew how the public would respond to a talking cartoon character.

But Walt, sure of his instinct, risked all the studio's money on his first sound cartoon. It wasn't easy. First he needed to find someone with the right equipment. He finally met a "big, lovable, friendly Irishman" named Pat Powers, who had developed a sound system for theaters. Walt also agreed to let Powers distribute the Mickey cartoons to theaters.

Walt then set out to produce the right sound effects. He hired thirty musicians and four sound-effects men and took them to a soundstage Powers had provided. The first session was a disaster, because nobody knew how to play "on cue," synchronized to what was happening on the screen. Walt then developed an original form of sheet music that helped everyone stay "in sync"—quite an accomplishment since Walt had no formal training in music.

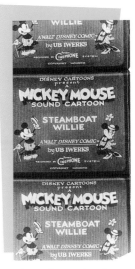

The title credits from *Steamboat Willie*, which was released prior to *Plane Crazy*

Finally, on November 18, 1928, *Steamboat Willie* opened at the Colony Theater in New York. It was an instant success. "It is an ingenious piece of work with a good deal of fun," wrote the *New York Times*, which also described its "mirthful quality."

Mickey Mouse took off like no other cartoon character had ever done.

In 1929, a cinema called the Fox Dome Theater in Ocean Park, California, started a Mickey Mouse Club for local children. Hundreds of kids applied to this fan club. Soon there were hundreds of other Mickey Mouse Clubs, with a combined membership of well over a million children. Over the course of the next decade or so, while

Mickey at the helm in *Steamboat Willie*, Walt's first cartoon "talkie"

developing new story ideas for Mickey, Walt and his animators came up with additional characters that soon became as popular as Mickey himself, including Donald Duck, Goofy, and Pluto.

Many people would have decided to play it safe and be content with just producing Mickey cartoons and making a lot of money. But not Walt. Walt always wanted to go for the next challenge, to push the boundaries, to see what new and exciting opportunity might lie over the horizon. "I wanted something different. And playing with music and doing things with music was intriguing. So I started the Silly Symphonies," Walt explained.

The Silly Symphonies were cartoons in which the stories were based on well-known works of music. Audiences loved them! Then, when Walt learned of a new process for making films in color, he immediately decided to take the bold step of making a color cartoon. It was a Silly Symphony named *Flowers and Trees*. The Hollywood film industry was so impressed with it that the Academy of Motion Picture Arts and Sciences gave Walt an Oscar—the first Academy Award ever given to a cartoon.

Curiously, even though the studio was doing so well, Roy couldn't quite make the books balance. He suspected that Pat Powers was keeping profits that should have gone to the studio. It turned out that things were even worse: Powers secretly went behind Walt and Roy's back and made an offer to Ub Iwerks to come and work for him, producing his own cartoon series, *Flip the Frog*. Ub accepted, and Walt was sad to see his old friend leave.

Powers wanted Walt to come to work for him, too, offering him the huge sum of $2,500 a week. But Walt refused. At least this time the character, Mickey Mouse, belonged to Walt.

Chapter 8

SNOW WHITE

Walt always loved children. In 1930, Lilly's sister Hazel and her daughter, Marjorie, moved in with Walt and Lilly. Walt enjoyed acting the role of father to Marjorie, who was a teenager at the time. If she came home late at night, Walt would be waiting for her at the top of the stairs. Walt and Lilly wanted to have children of their own, and in 1933 Lilly gave birth to a baby girl named Diane Marie.

Marjorie, Hazel, Walt, and Lilly at Los Feliz in the early 1930s

Like any other father, Walt wanted to surround his young daughter with beautiful things, but he tried hard not to spoil her. "Dad realized after a while that the more you want things, the better you like them," Diane said. Walt and Lilly wanted more children. Unfortunately, Lilly was unable to have more. So they decided to adopt a child, and in January 1937, Sharon Mae was brought home. Diane was terribly excited to have a baby sister.

Walt, Lilly, and baby Diane

While Walt's family grew, so did the Disney studio. Walt's animators had been using the Silly Symphony series to master many new techniques in animation, including techniques that improved the motion of human figures. As his artists became better at animating people, Walt began to think that Hollywood was ready for a giant step forward—a feature-length cartoon. Up until this time, cartoons were typically just short

Walt holding baby Sharon

films that appeared before the main movie. Today, of course, we are used to seeing animated features like *The Lion King* or *The Little Mermaid*. But, in the 1930s, the idea that audiences would want to sit through a full-length cartoon was very new. Many people in Hollywood didn't believe that families would buy tickets just to see a cartoon. Some even worried that a long cartoon would be bad for your eyes!

Roy and Lilly had doubts about Walt's idea, as well. The studio was doing well, but making a feature-length cartoon would cost at least half a million dollars. If the film failed, they worried it might mean the end of the studio.

But Walt knew that all he needed was a good story and the money to produce it. First, he settled on a classic fairy tale by the Brothers Grimm. "I don't know why I picked *Snow White*," Walt said many years later. "It's a thing I remembered as a kid. I saw a movie in Kansas City one time, it was *Snow White* with Marguerite Clark. . . . I thought it was a perfect story. It had the sympathetic dwarfs, . . . the "heavy," . . . the prince, and the girl. The romance."

Many of the animators remember how shocked they were when Walt brought them together and announced they were going to make a feature-length cartoon. Walt knew his staff was skeptical, so he acted out the entire story, as he pictured it in his mind. "He was a terrific actor," says Frank Thomas, one of the animators who worked on *Snow White*. "He would just say, 'The

Sharon (left) and Diane

queen gets up here and does this, and Snow White's down here. And she's singing 'Some Day,' and here comes the prince on his horse. . . . And he just acted out every part of it spontaneously." Before long, Walt's staff was excited, too, and they set to work.

From 1936 through 1937, Walt was completely absorbed in making *Snow White*. The studio added three hundred new artists. The cost of producing the film rose from half a million to about $1.5 million, which was a huge amount of money at the time. But while Walt's staff believed in the project, cynics outside the studio began talking about the *Snow White* production as "Disney's folly," and predicted that it would fail.

Walt simply plowed on, deeply involved in every aspect of the production. He sat in on story meetings, where the animators and writers came together and decided on important elements in the story. And often Walt had his animators revise their sketches again and again until they were just right.

Walt spent a lot of time on the music, too. He had no formal music training, but he had a natural talent for knowing what type of melody would work and which songs would

A sketch for the "Huntsman" scene in *Snow White*

Snow White . . .

. . . and the Dwarfs

Walt and Lilly at the
Snow White premiere

not. And he had a very clear sense about how Snow White should sound: He wanted a girl who could sing like a true soprano, but still had a childlike quality. After dozens of auditions he found Snow White in an eighteen-year-old singer named Adriana Caselotti, who had been trained by her family in Italian opera.

In the meantime, Walt and Roy made a deal with a new distributor, RKO, famous for its hit musicals—which they hoped *Snow White* would become. For the remainder of 1937, the staff at the Disney studio worked deep into the nights to finish the film. At long last, on December 21, 1937, *Snow White and the Seven Dwarfs* had its premiere at the Carthay Circle Theater. "It was a big, grand Hollywood premiere," Walt remembered later. "All the Hollywood brass turned out for my cartoon!"

Audiences as well as critics were full of praise for *Snow White*. Songs from the film, such as "Whistle While You Work," were played over and over on the radio. Meanwhile, money from *Snow White* box-office receipts poured into the studio. Walt used some of his new-found cash to put his animators back in art school to learn new techniques, so that he could make feature cartoons that were even better than *Snow White*. "We have worlds to conquer," he said.

Walt's faith in the animated feature had proved right. The studio would continue to turn out shorts for many years to come, but from that time on, the name "Disney" meant feature-length, animated films.

* * * * * * * *

Despite his success, Walt didn't live a typical Hollywood life full of glamorous parties. And he avoided publicity, preferring instead to be at home with his family. The girls had little idea their father was famous.

CalArts

Walt discussing CalArts with Mrs. Richard Van Hagen, one of the school's patrons

Walt always felt that young people should be encouraged to use their creative talents to the best of their ability. He didn't like the way most art schools only taught one subject, be it painting, music, or theater. Many years of making films had taught him that music, art, acting, and storytelling were intertwined—that you should not separate one from the other.

One of Walt's dreams was to build a school that would teach all these things to talented young men and women. When Walt was first starting out and couldn't afford to train his young animators, Mrs. Nelbert Chouinard, founder of the Chouinard Art Institute, had given them art lessons for free. Later, in the 1960s, when her school fell on hard times, Walt would have the chance to return her kindness: He came up with the idea to merge the Chouinard Art Institute with the Los Angeles Conservatory of Music, to create a new type of school where the arts—music, art, film, dance, and theater—could be explored together. When Walt died, he left half his estate to support the new school.

Due to his generosity, his dream would become a reality. Students from all over the United States, and even around the world, come to the California Institute of the Arts—"CalArts"—near Los Angeles to develop their creativity and be inspired by the legacy of one of the great visionaries of our time: Walt Disney.

"We weren't brought up with the idea that this was a great man," said Sharon. "He was just Daddy."

On weekends, Walt's family would often get together with his brothers' families for cookouts and croquet. Even though Walt got to see plenty of Roy and Herb, he missed his parents, who were still living in Portland, Oregon, with Ruth. Flora and Elias were getting older, and Flora's health was failing. So Walt and Roy invited their parents to come to Los Angeles—to enjoy the sunny California weather and watch their grandchildren grow up. Flora and Elias agreed, and the brothers bought them a house in North Hollywood.

Elias, Flora, and baby Diane, around 1933

The older couple was very happy with their new home, but they soon discovered that the gas furnace was not working properly. Walt sent some studio repairmen to fix it, but the problem didn't go away. On the morning of November 26, 1938, Elias woke up to find his wife's body on the bathroom floor. The furnace had been leaking deadly gas fumes into the house. Elias passed out while trying to carry her to another room. When help arrived, Elias was saved in the nick of time, but Flora had already died.

"It was frightful and really heartbreaking for Walt and Roy both," said Walt's niece Marjorie. Elias "was lost without" Flora, Walt said. "I never felt so sorry for anybody in my life as I did my Dad."

Walt himself never got over the tragedy. He was a man who enjoyed talking about his life—successes and failures alike—but he was never really able to talk about the loss of his mother.

Chapter 9

THE FIRST DISNEY CLASSICS

With the money from *Snow White,* Walt began to build a new studio in Burbank, big enough to support the production of twenty cartoon shorts and one major feature per year. He also wanted to create a workplace that would be pleasant—more like a college campus than an animation studio. The Burbank studio would have large rooms filled with natural light and a good restaurant where workers could eat their lunch. The animation building would even be equipped with an unheard-of luxury: air conditioning.

Walt acting out a scene for his animators in front of the *Pinocchio* storyboard

Meanwhile, Walt moved ahead with new feature films, beginning with *Pinocchio.* Naturally, Walt wanted to make the tale of the wooden puppet who comes to life even bigger and better than *Snow White.* The problem was that the original story of *Pinocchio,* based on an 1888 book by Collodi, did not have so many lovable characters as *Snow White.* Six months into the production, Walt, worried that he had a failure in the works, stopped work on the film and challenged his story writers to come up with ideas for improving it. The solution: Jiminy Cricket, a sidekick for Pinocchio, who could lend some zest and personality to the story.

Jiminy Cricket

At the same time as Walt's staff was working on *Pinocchio*, they ventured into a far more experimental film: *Fantasia*. The studio had been working on a Mickey Mouse cartoon based on the story of *The Sorcerer's Apprentice* when Walt met the famous conductor Leopold Stokowski, who offered to conduct the music for the

Pinocchio with Stromboli, the evil puppeteer

film. As work on the production progressed, *The Sorcerer's Apprentice* grew into a feature-length film called *Fantasia,* which was made up of eight separate pieces, including *The Sorcerer's Apprentice*.

Walt's idea was to use animation to bring pictures and music together in a whole new way. He, Stokowski, and his animators would sit together and think about what images came to mind

Mickey played the mischievous Sorcerer's Apprentice in *Fantasia*.

as they listened to music by Beethoven, Bach, and other composers. Did the music sound more "orange" or more "purple" to them? Did it make them think of dinosaurs? Or fairies? Or hippos wearing tutus? When Walt first heard a particular piece of the score with woodwinds, it made him think of "spaghetti floating around in a hot kettle."

Walt with a sketch from *Fantasia*

Because Walt always wanted to make things bigger and better, both *Pinocchio* and *Fantasia* cost more money than he and Roy had originally estimated. But because of the enormous success of *Snow White,* they weren't concerned. Then, in September 1939, Nazi Germany invaded Poland, launching World War II in Europe. With much of Europe deeply enmeshed in the conflict, Walt stopped getting the money he had been earning from theaters overseas.

When *Pinocchio* was finally ready for release in February 1940, the mood in America had also darkened. With the war raging, people were not as interested in seeing fairy tales in the movies as they had been in the days of *Snow White.*

Fantasia came out later that year. While some critics hailed it as a dazzling new approach to animation, others had trouble with its mix of cartoon characters and classical music. So *Pinocchio* and *Fantasia* lost money at the box office (although, over time, both films became successful Disney classics). As a result of these two pictures, and the cost of the new facility, the studio was again in debt. While employees were worried about their jobs, Walt was worried about having to lay off any of his employees.

The situation at the studio got even worse. Since Walt's staff had grown so much, he no longer had a personal relationship with each and every person on his payroll. So when rumors about layoffs began flying around the studio, many of Walt's employees were persuaded to join a union to protect their rights.

When Disney's lawyer and the union leaders couldn't come to terms, about 40 percent of the studio staff wound up going on strike, and many marched

Employees on strike outside the Disney studio

outside the studio in a picket line. They held signs that claimed Walt was a slave driver and shouted angrily at him as he drove in and out of the studio.

THE MULTIPLANE CAMERA

Even though animated drawings are flat, Walt wanted to give his feature cartoons the impression of depth—as though the camera taking the pictures was actually moving through space. The solution was an invention called the multiplane camera. It allowed animators to produce drawings on a series of separate glass plates. Each of these plates could move independently of the others. To imagine how it works, picture yourself looking out the window of a speeding train. The trees in the foreground move very fast, but a house in the distance stays in view for a long time, and a mountain on the horizon may not seem to move at all. The multiplane system allowed the animators to move objects in the foreground in different ways and at different speeds from objects in the background. The result was an illusion of real-world depth and distance. The multiplane camera had first been used in a 1937 short called *The Old Mill*, but it created its most spectacular effects to date in *Pinocchio*.

Animators at work using the multiplane camera

Meanwhile, many of Walt's artists crossed the picket line and went to work.

Soon after the strikers started picketing, the American government asked Walt to go on a goodwill tour of Latin America to help keep South Americans from joining Nazi Germany in the war. At first, Walt refused; he didn't think of himself as a politician. Then he was convinced that he could use the trip to do research for future films. The trip also gave him a chance to get away from the stressful atmosphere at the studio during the strike. So in 1941, Walt, Lilly, and a creative team from the studio spent a couple of months in South America.

Donald Duck and Aurora Miranda in *The Three Caballeros*

The fame of Mickey, Donald Duck, and Snow White had preceded them, and Walt and Lilly were received like royalty. Based on their experiences and the material they gathered there, Walt and his team produced a film called *Saludos Amigos* in 1943, followed by *The Three Caballeros* in 1945.

Although the trip was a great success, there was bad news from home while Walt was away: His father Elias died. At 82, Elias had never quite recovered from the death of his beloved wife. Walt was saddened to hear the news. He remarked, "I only wish that Roy and I could have had success sooner, so we could have done more for my mother and father."

During this same time, the strike at the studio was settled, with the studio giving in to much of what the

Dumbo, released in 1941, cost Disney a reasonable $812,000 to produce.

workers demanded. Although everyone was back to work, there remained a lot of bitterness between the staffers who had struck and those who had continued to go to work. Walt tried hard to forgive and forget, insisting, "We've had our differences on a lot of things, but we're going to continue making pictures, and we're going to find a way to work together." But Walt had been deeply hurt by his staff, and he and his creative people would never share the same close relationship they had prior to the strike.

WALT'S EARLY STEREOPHONIC SOUND

Two tutu-wearing hippos in the "Dance of the Flowers" in *Fantasia*

Because the music in *Fantasia* was so important, Walt wanted to give people in the movie theater the impression that they were listening in a live concert hall. He challenged his sound department to make this possible. The engineers knew that when we listen to concerts, each ear hears the sound slightly differently. They therefore split the soundtrack of *Fantasia* into two slightly different speaker channels. On the left side, you would hear the strings more clearly, and on the right side the brass section would be a bit louder—as if the instrument sections were seated to the left and right of you on a concert stage. It worked. By creating two channels, music gained a whole new sense of space, as if you were truly hearing it played live, rather than on a sound track. The result was an early version of what we call stereo sound, which Walt called the *Fantasound* system. Of course, all music today is recorded in stereo. But few people know that Walt was one of the first to experiment with this technology.

Chapter 10

THE STUDIO GOES TO WAR

On December 7, 1941, the Japanese bombed Pearl Harbor, and President Franklin Roosevelt told Americans that they had formally entered the war. The very next day, the U.S. Army told Walt that they would be taking over his studio. There was a Lockheed plant nearby that produced aircraft for the war, and the army wanted to make sure the area around it was protected—particularly since they feared the Japanese navy would attack the California coast.

A scene from Walt's wartime film *Victory Through Air Power*, which was based on a book by Major Alexander de Seversky

A few weeks later, Walt was asked to produce twenty short films for the U.S. Navy, to help teach the new American recruits how to recognize enemy planes. Soon, the studio started making hundreds of animated training films for the military, as well as producing films to inspire patriotism.

During the war, Walt stopped much of his usual work, with the notable exception of a feature about a young deer, called *Bambi*. To encourage the animators to make the animals as lifelike as possible, live animals were brought into the studio. Bambi, Thumper, and the other characters were as adorable as Walt had hoped,

An animator studies deer anatomy during the making of *Bambi*.

Bambi and his friend Thumper
sliding across a frozen pond

and the movie set a new standard for realism in animated pictures.

* * * * * * *

A perfectionist, Walt was both admired and feared by his staff. His artists called the rooms in which they screened films "sweatboxes," because Walt made them sweat over every frame. But as tough as he was at the studio, he was very different at home. "Dad was a very affectionate man," says his daughter Diane. "Whenever we'd walk anywhere with Dad, he'd always have his hand draped over our shoulders—Mother, Sharon, and me. He was a very warm human being."

All the way through high school, Walt drove his daughters to school. "We thought it would be a problem for him, because our schools were so far from where we lived," Diane says. "But, actually, he liked spending the extra time with us, and when he drove the long way back to the studio, he found it finally gave him some time to be alone and think.

"He liked the long drive so much that, one day, he said to Mother, 'We need to move, because I need more time in the car.' So that is when we planned to move from Los Feliz Hills, which was near the old Hyperion studio, to West Los Angeles. The freeways didn't exist then, so he had plenty of time to drive and think about what to do at the studio."

By 1949, Walt and Lilly had started to build their new house, on Carolwood Drive in Holmby Hills. They didn't want a big Hollywood mansion, but a home that would be easy to clean and maintain. Not that it was an ordinary house: It had a projection room where the family could watch the latest films and a playroom with a real soda fountain.

Ever since his childhood visits from Uncle Mike, Walt had been fascinated by trains. He was happy to find another train buff at the studio—Ward Kimball—who even had a barn with a real locomotive and a half-mile of track. Walt was determined to get his own railroad, too.

Lilly wasn't very happy with the idea of having a train running around her new house, so Walt laid the track in such a way that it did not obstruct the views from the house. The 2,615-foot track ran up hills and down through valleys, around curves, and even underground: There was a 120-foot-long, S-shaped tunnel, which ran right under Lilly's flower beds. Six years before he opened Disneyland, Walt had actually built his first thrill ride—at his own house!

Walt's giant train set ran past his workshop/barn.

At the studio, machinist Roger Broggie taught Walt to operate machine tools, and, before long, Walt and Broggie were building a train to one-eighth scale, which Walt called his "Carolwood Pacific Railroad." It had its maiden voyage shortly after the house was completed, with the entire work crew on board. To maintain his new railroad, Walt built a barn on the property that looked like the farm building in Marceline as he

Walt riding the "Carolwood Pacific Railroad" around his backyard

remembered it. The barn became Walt's machine shop, where he would work until late in the night.

Chapter 11

LIVE-ACTION FILMS

Walt and the studio had taken a break from animated features during the war, in order to concentrate on films for the U.S. military. When the war ended, the studio was in debt once again, because it had charged the U.S. government for little more than the cost of production, not taking into account the cost of running the studio. Roy told Walt that there was no way

Pluto encounters an angry bulldog in *Bone Trouble* (1940).

the studio could continue work on big features like *Peter Pan* and *Alice in Wonderland,* which had been in early development in 1941. As a result, Walt was forced to go back to his roots and produce animated shorts featuring famous Disney characters such as Mickey Mouse, Donald Duck, and Pluto. Although these projects earned some money for the studio, the work wasn't enough of a challenge for Walt. He was looking to do something new.

Walt sent a husband-and-wife team of photographers, Alfred and Alma Milotte, to Alaska to film seals. They returned with miles of film, which many people at the studio thought was the most boring footage in the world.

One of the stars of *Seal Island*

But Walt saw potential where others saw acres of lazy seals. He had the material edited to form a storyline that, accompanied by music, kept audiences spellbound. The result was a half-hour documentary called *Seal Island.*

Now, with entire cable TV channels devoted to nature films, the idea of a film about animals seems unremarkable. But in the 1940s nature films were unheard of. As had happened so many times in the past, Walt's distributor, RKO, did not want to bring this unusual film to theaters. Walt responded by running the film in a local theater near Los Angeles, so that it would qualify for the Academy Awards.

Seal Island won the Academy Award for Best Documentary of 1948. Holding the Oscar in his hands, Walt told Roy, "Now, go hit the guys at RKO over the head with it." The success of *Seal Island* meant that Walt could continue to make similar films, which he called True-Life Adventures.

A poster for *Seal Island*, the first of the True-Life Adventures

* * * * * * * * *

Walt was also interested in pursuing live-action films—those that used real actors rather than animated cartoons. The first film he made with no animation at all was *Treasure Island,* based on the novel by Robert Louis Stevenson. Walt insisted that his live-action features be made with the same care as his animated films. He always planned a cartoon in the form of a series of drawings, each representing an important moment in the film. Walt would pin these drawings to a big board—a "storyboard"—so that he and his staff could look at the entire story all at once. Walt expected his staff to create storyboards for live-action films, too, so that he could ensure that he and his producers agreed on what the film would look like before he sent them off to film it on location. The storyboard, Walt's creation, is now used in the production of all major Hollywood films.

Treasure Island was shot in British studios and on location on the Cornish coast of England. Walt took his family to visit the sets, where they met the British cast and delighted in the glamour of real, live-action

Cinderella releases her furry friend Gus from a mousetrap.

Walt, Diane, and Sharon with actor Bobby Driscoll (far left) on the set of *Treasure Island*

Walt on the set of *20,000 Leagues*

filmmaking. The experience energized Walt. When he returned to Los Angeles, he teased his animators about it. "Actors are great," he said. "You give 'em the lines, they rehearse a couple of times, and you've got it on film—it's finished. You guys—you take six months to draw a scene!"

At the same time, the studio completed the first animated feature since the war: *Cinderella,* Walt's return to a fairy tale filled with adventure and romance. Audiences loved the film, and it became one of the most successful films of 1950.

But after the *Treasure Island* experience, Walt's attention was more focused on the potential of live-action films. He decided to shoot three more adventure films in England: *The Story of Robin Hood and His Merrie Men* (1952), *The Sword and the Rose* (1953), and *Rob Roy the Highland Rogue* (1954). Then, after four successes in five years, Walt set his mind on his biggest live-action project to date: *20,000 Leagues Under the Sea,* based on the story by Jules Verne.

Walt looked forward to the technical challenge of filming the underwater adventures of a big submarine, but he was worried about how Roy would react to the idea. He knew it could cost well over $3 million to produce. Much to his surprise, Roy was supportive. "As time went on," Walt

The squid attacks in *20,000 Leagues.*

remembered, "I had to go see him and say, 'Roy, it looks like it's going to be another $300,000.' And still he just nodded and smiled." Roy was smiling even when Walt's budget hit $4 million. Roy was right to have faith. With amazing special effects and big stars like Kirk Douglas, James Mason, and Peter Lorre, *20,000 Leagues* became a huge hit when it was released in 1954. Filmed in the new, wide-screen CinemaScope format, it announced to Hollywood that Walt Disney was a major force in the big business of making live-action movies.

"PLUSSING"

In the music accompanying this scene from *Cinderella*, a different harmony is added with each new bubble.

Walt had a natural curiosity and was always looking to make things better and more interesting. He called the process "plussing," and it applied to everything in his films, from camera shots to special effects to dialogue and music. One particularly memorable example of plussing came during the creation of *Cinderella*.

"We had just recorded a song when Walt came in and listened to it," says Ilene Woods, the voice of Cinderella. "When it was over, he looked up and said, 'Ilene, can you sing harmony with yourself?' What he meant was, can you sing many different versions of the song, listening to yourself on tape through headphones?" Then Walt directed the engineer to record the same song several times, with Ilene singing a different song part in harmony each time. Of course these days many performers use modern recording equipment to sing harmony with themselves. But Walt was the first to come up with the idea.

Ilene Woods recording a song for *Cinderella*

Chapter 12

WALT'S KINGDOM

The carousel at Griffith Park in Los Angeles

Having achieved enormous success producing animated and live-action features, Walt Disney still longed for new challenges. "The idea for Disneyland started when my daughters were very young," said Walt. "Sunday was always Daddy's day with the two daughters." Often, they wound up in Los Angeles's Griffith Park, home of a particularly beautiful carousel with hand-carved horses.

"I'd sit there, eating peanuts, while they rode the merry-go-round and did all these things," Walt remembered. "I felt that there should be something built, some kind of an amusement enterprise, where the parents and the children could have fun together." And that's how it all began—with a merry-go-round, a bench, and a bag of peanuts.

In 1948, Walt wrote down some early thoughts for a theme park. He was thinking of putting it across Riverside Drive from the studio. That way he could take advantage of the numbers of tourists who were interested in seeing how a real Hollywood studio worked. "The Main Village, which includes the Railway Station, is built around a village green," Walt wrote. "In this park, there will be benches, a bandstand, drinking fountain, trees and shrubs. . . . Around the park will be the town."

Soon Walt began to think of his amusement park as a far grander project—separate from what was happening at the studio. Some years before,

Walt and Roy had sold stock in their company. So even though they ran the company, they didn't entirely own it. And Roy was very concerned that the other stockholders wouldn't approve of the idea of a film

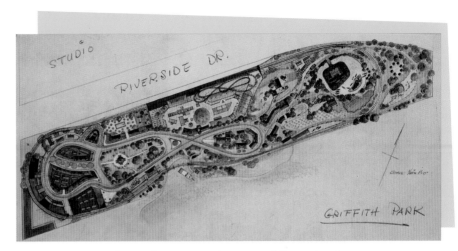

An early concept drawing of Disneyland

studio going out and opening an amusement park. So at first, Walt didn't have use of the company's funds.

Walt was undeterred: He borrowed money from his own life insurance and gathered a small staff in a new company to help him develop his initial ideas. The company became WED Enterprises (short for Walter Elias Disney). When WED needed more money, Walt sold his vacation home in Palm Springs. Many of his staff invested their own money in the park as well, and Roy eventually began to see the project in a different light. Even with this support, Walt was still short of the money he'd need.

Determined to build his dream park, Walt finally hit upon the solution: television. At that point in the early 1950s, the big Hollywood studios had tried hard to ignore this new invention. They worried that people would stay home to watch free programs on TV rather than coming to a movie theater where they'd have to buy a ticket. But Walt saw a unique opportunity. Television networks like NBC, ABC, and CBS were still small, and they were desperate for the kind of entertainment that only a studio like Disney could make. Of the three, ABC was the newest, smallest, and under the greatest pressure to compete with its rivals.

Having already produced two Christmas television specials, Walt now came up with the idea of producing a weekly show. Walt liked the freedom television gave him. "If I had an idea for some film, I had to go and try to sell it to the distributors, to the theater men, and everyone else. With television, I just get my gang together and we say this will be something interesting—let's do it. And I take that direct to the public," he explained.

Walt in a television lead-in for an episode of "Disneyland"

So Roy traveled to New York and completed a deal with ABC. Walt would produce a weekly show for them, and, in turn, ABC would put money into Disneyland. Soon thereafter, the first "Disneyland" television show came on the air. The show's theme varied from week to week: In one episode, Davy Crockett would be fighting the Indians; the following week would feature polar bears in the snow; next, the show might visit Disneyland and offer a peek at the newest attractions under construction. Naturally, this created a lot of excitement around the opening of the park. What's more, Walt himself presented the show, making his face as famous as his name.

In August 1954, construction workers began excavations for Disneyland—with the scheduled opening less than eleven months away! The plans called for four large "lands" with attractions inspired by Disney films. Adventureland was inspired by Walt's True-Life Adventure films, and included Jungle Cruise. Fantasyland would have a series of rides based on Disney animated classics such as *Dumbo* and *Peter Pan*. Frontierland would hark back to the days of the Wild West and include a big paddle-wheeled steamboat, the *Mark Twain*. And, finally, Tomorrowland would show a glimpse of the future, complete with a Rocket to the Moon ride—even though, in 1954, the United States had yet to build a rocket that could fly into space, and was still fifteen years away from

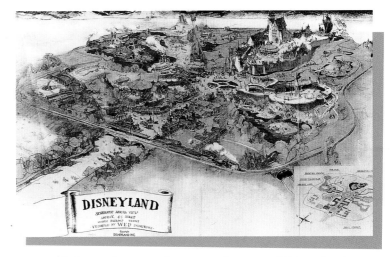

Herb Ryman's original concept drawing of Disneyland

landing on the moon. Sleeping Beauty Castle stood at the center of these four lands, and Main Street ran between the park's entrance and the castle.

Of course, nobody had ever built a place like this before. Walt and his designers had to figure out how to do it as they went along. He had planned to

Sleeping Beauty Castle under construction in 1955

populate his Jungle Cruise with live animals, but experts told him that big game like lions, tigers, and hippos sleep through much of the day and only come out at night. In other words, the riders on the cruise boats would rarely glimpse an animal. So Walt asked his WED engineers—he called them "Imagineers" —to develop mechanical animals. Every passenger on each cruise boat, at any time of day, would be assured of seeing the wildlife in simulated form.

53

AUDIO-ANIMATRONICS

Walt in the Tiki Room

Audio-Animatronics was one of the technologies Walt's engineers experimented with for the New York World's Fair. Through an intricate mechanism controlled by an early kind of computer, Walt's designers could make animal figures move and behave as if they were real.

The first Audio-Animatronics figures were the birds of the Tiki Room in Disneyland. For the World's Fair, Walt wanted to create a life-size figure that would act just as if it were a real human being. Walt chose one of his heroes, President Abraham Lincoln. The WED team programmed the figure to act and speak in such a lifelike way that many people thought it was a real man. Walt never lost his enthusiasm for the Mr. Lincoln show. "I think every time he sat through it, he cried," said his daughter Sharon. "The speech was so good."

The Audio-Animatronics® Mr. Lincoln

Walt insisted that the park be absolutely spotless and safe. Herb Ryman, the artist who created the first full-blown sketch of the park, remembered that "whenever Walt went down on a tour of inspection, one of the first things he'd do is go into the restrooms to see that everything was working."

Several days before Disneyland opened, Walt and Lilly celebrated their thirtieth anniversary there in the Golden Horseshoe saloon. It was a memorable night for the entire family. Walt and Lilly were dancing on the stage, and Walt was as happy as a kid during a birthday party. On the way home, Diane recalls that her father was sitting in the backseat of the car, holding a rolled-up Disneyland map and "tooting through it like a little boy with a toy trumpet."

Disneyland's opening day, July 17, 1955, was televised, live, in a ninety-minute program on ABC. It was the most-watched television event of that time. Hosted by Art Linkletter, Bob Cummings, and future president Ronald Reagan, the show gave America a first glimpse of all the exciting things that awaited them in Disneyland.

Viewers thought that the park's first day went without a hitch, but in truth, "It was a great mishmash of last-minute things that hadn't been done," remembers Art Linkletter. "The cement wasn't hardened in some places. Piles of lumber were here and there, and trees that had died had been repainted green, instead of watered." What's more, fake entrance tickets overloaded the park with unexpected guests.

Soon enough, the problems in the park were fixed and the original set of attractions completed. But Walt had no intention of leaving Disneyland the way it was. He wanted to keep adding attractions and to make it better each year. Several years later, he opened the 20,000 Leagues Under the Sea exhibit, based on the movie. A whole parade of notables and navy officers attended the event. And when Walt unveiled the most futuristic attraction of all, the new Monorail train, then–Vice President Richard Nixon came down for the first ride.

Vice President Richard Nixon and his family came to Disneyland for the opening of the Monorail in 1959.

Chapter 13

A WONDERFUL WORLD

Walt with Ron and Diane on their wedding day

In the early 1950s, Walt's children went off to college: Diane studied at University of Southern California, and Sharon went to the University of Arizona. While at USC, Diane met a tall and handsome football player named Ron Miller. They were married in 1954.

When their first baby, Christopher, arrived at the end of the year, Walt was overjoyed to have a grandson in the family, though he was disappointed that the child wasn't named after him. He had to wait six more years before Diane gave birth to another boy—the fifth of her seven children. She named him Walter Elias Disney Miller, and Walt promptly passed out cigars printed with the name of his new grandson.

Sharon married an architect named Robert Brown on May 10, 1959, in Pacific Palisades. Eventually, both Ron Miller and Bob Brown went to work for Walt: Ron at the studio, and Bob at WED.

Walt holding his grandson Chris

At the same time, Walt's professional life continued to thrive. The "Disneyland" show on ABC, which he hosted, was a roaring success. Early on, Walt had made the decision to film his television shows in color. This was surprising, because none of the networks were broadcasting in color yet.

Walt simply knew that the additional cost was worthwhile and that someday it would pay off. And that it did.

Walt had shot three one-hour episodes of "Davy Crockett" with stars Fess Parker and Buddy Ebsen. The show was one of the biggest hits in the history of television. No ten-year-old in the country was fashionable if he or she didn't have a coonskin cap like Davy. Its theme music, sung by Parker, became a major hit, too. Since Walt had shot these programs in color, he was able to easily transfer the three one-hour television shows to movie theaters, where viewers could see "Davy Crockett" in color for the first time.

Fess Parker (right), TV's Davy Crockett, joins Walt on a ride down Main Street.

Early on, ABC had asked Walt to come up with a second show, just for children. For more than a year, he shaped an idea for a show that would not only be *for* kids but also presented *by* kids. "The Mickey Mouse Club" went on the air for the first time on October 3, 1955. Soon, millions of American children looked forward to daily visits with famous Mouseketeers like Annette Funicello, Sharon Baird, and Bobby Burgess, and their adult leaders, Jimmie Dodd and Roy Williams.

Walt seemed to have a magic touch with television. "The Mickey Mouse Club" became a major

Mouseketeer Bobby Burgess remembered of the other mouseketeers, "We were all good friends."

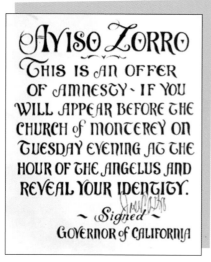

A prop poster from "Zorro"

Walt was very excited about the development of color television.

hit. From 1957 through 1959, he produced "Zorro," starring Guy Williams, which was also very popular. And "Disneyland" (retitled "Walt Disney Presents" in 1958) was still going strong. In 1961, after seven seasons on ABC, Walt moved over to NBC, in large part because he was intrigued by the network's lead in the development of color television. And on September 24, 1961, Walt launched "Walt Disney's Wonderful World of Color" on NBC.

Throughout the late 1950s and early 1960s, Walt continued to make live-action films, including *Old Yeller, Darby O'Gill and the Little People, Swiss Family Robinson, Pollyanna*, and *The Shaggy Dog*. Through the 1960s, the studio continued with a series of light-hearted comedies including *The Absent-Minded Professor, The Parent Trap, Son of Flubber*, and *That Darn Cat*.

Walt pitching hay in a TV lead-in

Somehow, during this same period, Walt found time to work on animated features as well. Encouraged by the success of *Cinderella*, Walt had finally been able to complete

A scene from *Son of Flubber,* the sequel to *The Absent-Minded Professor*

Hayley Mills, who became an overnight sensation in *Pollyanna,* played twin sisters in *The Parent Trap.*

Alice in Wonderland in 1951. In 1953, the studio released *Peter Pan,* and, in July 1955, *Lady and the Tramp* appeared in theaters nationwide. All were hits. Emboldened by success, Walt wanted his next animated feature to be the biggest and best of them all.

Walt decided it would be based on the famous fairy tale of Sleeping Beauty. He selected a young singer named Mary Costa as the voice of Princess Aurora. *Sleeping Beauty* cost more than $6 million to produce, which made it the most expensive animated film Walt had ever made. Audiences flocked to see the picture, but it didn't make enough money to cover the cost of production. The same year, the live-action film *The Shaggy Dog* took in about $8 million, and it had only cost $1 million to produce. Walt realized that whereas live-action films were perhaps more profitable in the short term, only the Disney studio was able to make the type of feature-length animated films that had made it famous. So both types of film would continue to be important for the long-term success of the studio.

Chapter 14

THE LAST DECADE

Walt with Julie Andrews (left) and
P. L. Travers at the premiere of
Mary Poppins

As Walt entered his sixties, he was as busy as ever.

He served as Pageantry Chairman for the 1960 Olympics in Squaw Valley, California. The following year, Walt told his designers at WED that they were going to work on the upcoming World's Fair in New York. A number of American companies had approached Walt to design attractions for their exhibits, or "pavilions," at the Fair. Says Imagineer John Hench, "No one could understand why he wanted to dabble in exhibitions for the World's Fair. We had our hands full with the studio and Disneyland, and suddenly he took on something that was full of risks and very little profit."

But Walt had three very good reasons: The World's Fair would give him the chance to see if Disneyland-type attractions would be as successful in the eastern part of the country as in California, since he was already thinking of building a theme park on the east coast. Second, he knew he would be able to develop all kinds of exciting new technology with the money from these corporations. Finally, he planned to design rides and attractions that later, after the fair had closed, could be brought back to Disneyland.

WED developed exhibits for the Ford Motor Company, General Electric, and the State of Illinois. Then, less than a year before the fair opened, the people from Pepsi-Cola called on Walt to see if he could develop an attraction for their pavilion, dedicated to UNICEF, the United Nations International Childrens' Emergency Fund. WED Imagineer Rolly Crump remembers the day very well. "He came in and said, 'I want to do a little boat ride for children.'" The Imagineers worked day and night for almost nine months, and the result was one of the most popular rides Walt had ever designed—"It's a Small World."

While Walt was overseeing the World's Fair, he became involved in his most ambitious film undertaking of all, *Mary Poppins*. Actually, it was his daughter Diane who, when she was a little girl, had introduced him to the original *Mary Poppins* book, by P. L. Travers, about the adventures of a mysterious nanny.

Walt pulled out all the stops. He chose Julie Andrews for the title role and wanted Dick Van Dyke for the role of Bert. "He was like a kid, he was so excited about it," Dick Van Dyke remembers. "And by the time I left him I was excited about it."

The songs for *Mary Poppins* were written by two brothers, Richard and Robert Sherman, and included such favorites as "A Spoonful of Sugar" and "Supercalifragilisticexpialidocious." *Mary Poppins* was a big hit at the box office, earning some $44 million during its original release—and five Oscars.

Dick Van Dyke dancing with animated penguins in *Mary Poppins*

In August 1966, Walt asked his daughters and their families to join him on a cruise through the waters of British Columbia, Canada. Although no one suspected it at the time, it was to be Walt's last big vacation with his whole family. He relaxed on deck by reading books about city planning, and made home movies of his grandchildren whenever they docked and explored the countryside.

Walt and Lilly with their grandchildren on his final family trip, a cruise through British Columbia

In the fall of 1966, Walt went to the hospital to be treated for an old neck injury. When the doctors took X-rays of his upper body, they discovered that he had lung cancer. He had smoked cigarettes all his life; now, the habit had finally caught up with him. Walt told his family that they shouldn't be concerned. He'd have the cancer removed and expected to recover fully. But it wasn't to be. After the surgery, the surgeon told Lilly, Diane, and Sharon that the cancer had spread and that Walt had only six months to two years to live.

Walt spent most of the next few weeks with his family, making plans for the future. "I'm going to concentrate on building EPCOT," he told his son-in-law, Ron. But on December 15, 1966, at age 65, he died. The flag at Disneyland flew at half-staff. Echoing sentiments all over the world, his old friend Joe Grant said, "It is the end of an era."

EPCOT

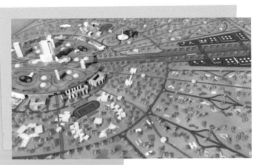

An aerial drawing of EPCOT

Walt really wanted to apply his lifetime of experience to create a new type of a city—one that was more livable, safe, and clean. This experimental city would also be a kind of greenhouse where American companies could try out new technologies, from toasters to refrigerators, from modern cars to new ways for removing trash and moving people around.

He studied, planned, sketched ideas, and purchased many acres of land in Florida—an area twice as big as Manhattan Island—for what was originally called "The Florida Project." Eventually, the concept became EPCOT, for the Experimental Prototype Community of Tomorrow.

Sadly, Walt wouldn't live to see his dream realized. His brother Roy, however, used the land he had purchased to build the Walt Disney World Resort. Today, EPCOT is more like a world's fair, including large exhibits sponsored by corporations, and a showcase of international pavilions, each dedicated to a particular country.

EPCOT at sunset

Walt measuring himself against a map of EPCOT

APPENDIX: IDEAS FOR FURTHER READING

BOOKS

Fanning, Jim, and Leeza Gibbons. *Walt Disney*. New York: Chelsea House, 1994.

Ford, Barbara. *Walt Disney: A Biography*. New York: Walker & Company, 1989 (out of print).

Green, Amy Boothe, and Howard E. Green. *Remembering Walt: Favorite Memories of Walt Disney*. New York: Hyperion, 1999.

Greene, Katherine, and Richard Greene. *Inside the Dream: The Personal Story of Walt Disney*. New York: Disney Editions, 2001.

Greene, Katherine, and Richard Greene. *The Man Behind the Magic: The Story of Walt Disney*. New York: Viking Penguin, 1998.

Thomas, Bob. *Walt Disney: An American Original*. New York: Hyperion, 1994.

WEB SITES

www.Disney.com

This site has the most comprehensive information about Disney films, theme parks, holidays, and merchandise.

www.Disney.go.com/Disneyland

This is the official Web site of Disneyland. You can visit the park's "lands," as well as the new Disney's California Adventure© theme park.

www.waltdisney.com

A virtual museum about Walt Disney developed by the Walt Disney Family Foundation, this site is filled with interesting stories and anecdotes about Walt. It also has special exhibits and film clips that change each month.